Miss
Gordon

# THE
# VICTORIANS

## Peter Hicks

**Wayland**

## Look into the Past

Series editor: Joanna Bentley
Series designer: David West
Book designer: Stephen Wheele

This edition published in 1998 by Wayland Publishers Ltd

First published in 1995 by Wayland Publishers Ltd,
61 Western Road, Hove, East Sussex, BN3 1JD, England

© Copyright 1995 Wayland Publishers Ltd

**British Library Cataloguing in Publication Data**
  Hicks, Peter
  Victorians. - (Look into the Past series)
  I.Title II.Series
  941.081

ISBN 0 7502 2562 9

Typeset by Dorchester Typesetting Group Ltd,
Dorset, England
Printed and bound in Italy by L.E.G.O. S.p.A., Vicenza, Italy

**Picture acknowledgements**
The publishers wish to thank the following for supplying the
photographs for this book: Brighton Reference Library 25
(bottom); Mary Evans Picture Library cover, 4, 9 (top), 12
(bottom), 13 (bottom), 17 (bottom), 22 (top), 23 (both), 27
(bottom) 28; Peter Hicks 11 (bottom), 15 (bottom), 20
(both), 24 (top), 25 (top); The Billie Love Collection 5 (top
right and bottom), 14, 17 (top), 18 (both), 21, 22 (bottom),
26 (top), 29 (both); The Mansell Collection 5 (top left), 13
(top), 26 (bottom); Norfolk Museums Service cover; Ann
Ronan at Image Select 6 (both), 10, 19, 24 (bottom);
Wayland Picture Library 8 (top), 9 (bottom), 15 (top), 16
(top), 27 (top).

# CONTENTS

Words that appear in ***bold italic*** in the text are explained in the glossary on page 30.

# WHO WERE THE VICTORIANS?

**People who lived in Britain during the reign of Queen Victoria (1837–1901) are often called 'Victorians'. This is a useful label for *historians*, but it suggests that everybody did and believed the same things. In fact, Victorians were very different: some were rich, some were poor; some worked and some did not. Life in Victorian Britain was not the same for everyone.**

By the time Victoria became Queen, Britain had been undergoing great changes. The ***Industrial Revolution***, which began after the 1760s, had created large towns and cities packed with mills, factories, warehouses, docks, canals and people. Britain no longer depended on farming for its wealth, but manufacturing – that is, making things. It was a very exciting time, but as we shall see, some people did better than others.

▲
The problem was that this Industrial Revolution had made Britain a very unequal country and by the nineteenth century there was a huge divide between rich and poor. The two women and the child you can see out walking come from rich families. Their clothes are made of the finest materials and in the latest fashion of the 1870s.

Despite the problems that faced Britain ▶ during this time, the Victorians are famous for their buildings and *engineering*. This is the Saltash Railway Bridge over the River Tamar in Devon. This bridge, which linked Cornwall to London by rail, was designed by the most famous Victorian engineer, Isambard Kingdom Brunel. He had to build it high, so that big ships – you can see one in the picture – could pass underneath.

▲
However, large numbers of people lived in dreadful poverty, usually because of low pay. The family in this picture have very little money. They have probably been thrown out of their home because they have been unable to pay the **rent**. Their clothes are little better than rags and will not keep out the cold and wet.

# WORK

**For ordinary people in Victorian Britain, the world of work was very hard. They worked long hours, often for low wages, with only one day off a week (Sunday). If they became sick, unemployed or too old to work there were no benefits as we have today. Families often put their children to work because they needed extra money to live. Employers liked to use children in factories because they were small and quick enough to clean machines without having to turn them off.**

One industry which ▶ employed many children was coal mining. Coal was very important because it ran the steam engines that drove the machines in factories and mills. It also powered the new steam locomotives and ships. Look at the pictures. *Parliament* was so shocked by such conditions that it passed a law in 1842 forbidding all women and children under ten from working in the coal mines. The work was very hard and dangerous. Look at the miner cutting, or 'hewing', coal. Pit ponies pulled the trucks, but the coal was cut by sheer muscle power.

Another industry ▶ that made Britain wealthy was the *textile* industry. Cotton was made in the mills of Lancashire and woollen cloth in Yorkshire. The making of cloth involved combing, spinning and weaving. Life was hard for textile workers, who spent at least twelve hours a day on their feet. Although women – often used as spinners – did the same work as men, they were paid less!

Iron was another product constantly needed for making things. The men who worked in the iron *foundries* also faced poor conditions and dangers. Look carefully at the ironworks. The huge machine is a steam hammer, and the men are helping to shape a large bar of red-hot iron. ▼

By 1867, Parliament had passed a number of laws that reduced the hours for children in mines and factories. But even the 'Ten hours a Day' Act still allowed children to work 58 hours a week! However, many children worked in small workshops or at home and had no protection from these laws. Look at this brickmakers' yard. The two workers are young girls. They were expected to work for very long hours. The air in these yards was very dusty and dangerous to young lungs.

In Victorian Britain, if you were a skilled worker and employers needed your skill, your wages were good. However, large numbers of people were unskilled and their wages were very low. Many unskilled women were employed by wealthy people as domestic servants. At any time in Victoria's reign there were over a million of them. The servants on the left worked incredibly long hours, carrying out boring and dirty jobs for very low wages and hardly any time off.

Another low-paid area of work was the 'sweated industries' like clothing manufacture. Based in thousands of workshops all over Britain, the women had no protection from labour laws. They were employed to stitch expensive clothes for the rich, while they were paid very low wages. It was backbreaking and painful work, especially when they sewed for a 15-hour shift.

One way that workers improved their ▶ conditions at work was through trade unions. A trade union is a group of workers, often from the same industry, who join together to try to increase their wages, make their work safer and reduce the number of hours they work. In Victoria's reign the first successful unions were for skilled workers like engineers. You can see a membership card for the 'Amalgamated Society of Engineers'.

# CITY LIFE

By 1851, for the first time in history, more British people lived in towns and cities than the countryside. This meant one of the main problems was overcrowding. The population of many towns and cities tripled during Victoria's reign, and many of them could not cope with the large numbers of people. Despite this, people were keen to live in towns because of the wide choice of jobs. However, as we shall see, for most of Victoria's reign, British cities were unpleasant places to live in.

Because so many ▶ people crowded into industrial cities such as Manchester, Leeds and Birmingham, the existing housing became badly overcrowded. Many families had to share rooms with others. Look at the 'Seven Dials' area of London. This was an area famous for second-hand shoes. Can you see them laid out for sale? The street is so crowded the cab can hardly make its way through.

One common style of housing was the back-to-back terraced housing which you can see in the picture. Each house had two rooms downstairs and two upstairs, and one back wall was the back wall of another house. This meant they were never properly *ventilated* and became very damp. These houses were built with cheap materials and had no running water, bathrooms or sewers, except for the open ditch in the front.

If you were wealthy or comfortably off you would live in what were called suburbs – cleaner districts further out from the grimy city centres. The factories and crowded houses made city centres unpleasant, so large houses were built where there was space and clean air. The type of house in the picture was built for a large, wealthy family with at least six servants.

Despite the smells and the dirt, large numbers of people preferred the city because there was so much more to do. There were well stocked shops, markets and street sellers, hundrcds of pubs, dances, theatres and most importantly, company. ▶

One special attraction came to London in 1851 – the Great Exhibition. A huge iron and glass building was built in Hyde Park to house an exhibition showing products and inventions from many nations of the world. It was the idea of Prince Albert, the husband of Queen Victoria. It was a great success, with 6 million people coming from all over Britain, many travelling on the new steam trains. There were special cheap entry days to allow poorer people to see the exhibition. ▼

Because many of the towns and cities of Victorian Britain contained hundreds of factories, air pollution was a serious problem. The factories were powered by steam engines, which constantly poured smoke into the air. You can see the effects of this in the picture of Sheffield in Yorkshire. Notice the tall chimneys and filthy clouds hanging over much of the city.

With thousands of ▶ people crammed together in the cities, crime was very common. It was easy for criminals to disappear into the crowd. Burglaries and street crime kept the new police forces very busy. When policemen first appeared in cities many ordinary people did not like them because they seemed to be on the side of the wealthy, but in time the 'bobby on the beat' was accepted.

# TRANSPORT

**People in Victorian Britain could travel more easily than ever before. In earlier times, people lived close to their work and did not have to walk far. Cities and towns were fairly *compact* because of this. However, with the introduction of horse drawn buses and trams and steam trains, people began to live further away from their work. As methods of transport improved the cities spread outwards and became busier.**

The steam train ▶ did change people's lives. At first only the rich travelled on this new invention, but cheaper fares did come, and it was possible for less wealthy people to travel by train. Look at the London and Birmingham railway terminus at Euston Square in London. Can you see the difference between the carriages? Obviously a ticket for an open truck was cheaper than one for a covered carriage.

▲ The introduction of the horse-drawn bus – the omnibus – in the early nineteenth century was the beginning of public transport in our cities. However, these could not take many passengers because of the weight. The horse-drawn tram was a great improvement because it ran on rails. Look carefully at the picture of Princes Street in Edinburgh and you can see both tram and bus. Which could carry more passengers? Because the tram ran on rails there was less work for the horses to do, and they could pull heavier loads. Notice the upstairs and driver's seat are not covered. This must have been uncomfortable during cold and wet weather!

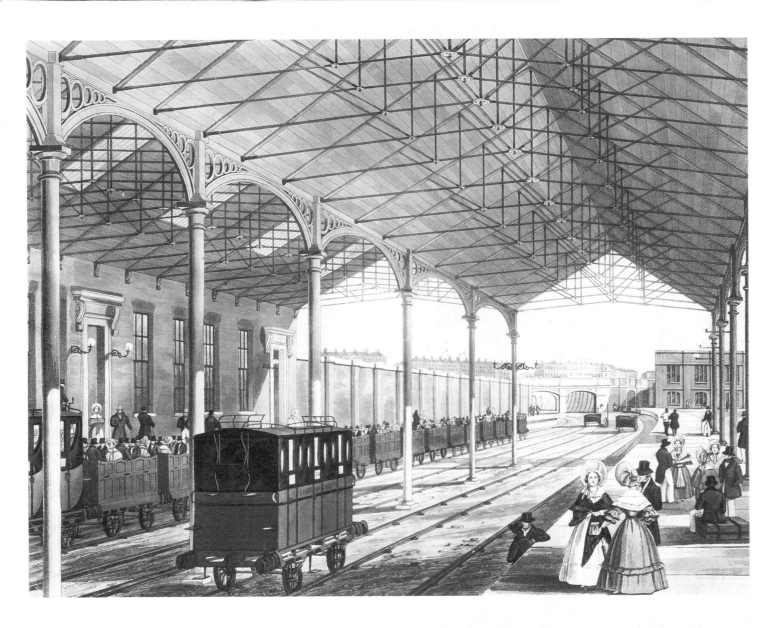

As the railway lines spread out from the cities, railway stations were built along them. Soon houses appeared around them and the railway suburbs were born. Many people preferred living away from the city centres and journeying to work by train. Railways not only changed our cities but also changed how Victorians worked. Seaside towns grew up and the habit of taking holidays began.

Look at the impressive **viaduct** in the picture. ▶ It carries the main line from London to Brighton. Victorian engineers did not allow problems like valleys to stop the railway!

One way the Victorians tried to overcome crowded streets was by going underneath them! In the 1860s the world's first underground railway was opened in London. Look at the picture of its construction and you can see how it was done. The road was dug up and a tunnel 6.5 m deep was built. The underground trains were pulled by steam, so the air must have been very smoky. By the 1890s underground lines were deeper, cleaner and faster, using electric trains. ▼

▲ Although railways did speed up life, movement in towns and cities depended on the speed of the horse. Look at the busy picture of Fleet Street in London. There are horse drawn vehicles of many different types. We often think that traffic jams came with the motor car, but Victorians complained of their horse drawn jams too. City streets were not designed for so much traffic, and cross town travel took a very long time.

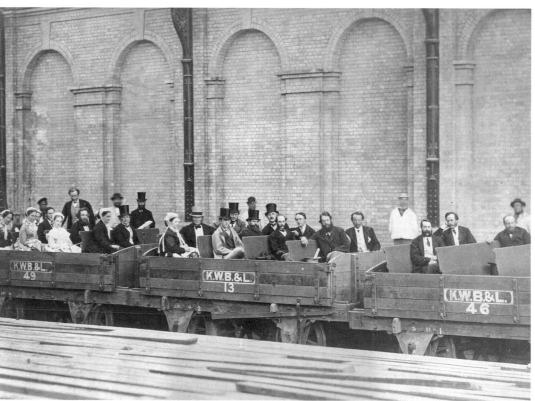

# COUNTRY LIFE

**Victorian paintings of country life often show neat fields and pretty cottages. The quality of life in the country depended on how wealthy you were. There were those who owned the land, those who rented it and those who worked on it, and all these people's experiences were very different.**

The life of the ▶ landowner and his family was very comfortable. Landowners earned a lot of money from the produce they sold, but also from the rents of *tenant farmers* who they let land to. As Britain's population rose and the cities grew bigger there was a huge demand for farm produce. This meant big profits for the landowners. Look at the country house in the picture. It looks wealthy and comfortable. Although the photograph was taken in August it is interesting to see how much clothing people wore.

▼ For tenant farmers life until the 1880s was good too. They made improvements to their farms and some were able to buy machinery, like the reaper to help in harvesting. The coming of the railways helped many farms. Produce such as milk, fresh vegetables and livestock could be sent quickly and cheaply to nearby towns and cities.

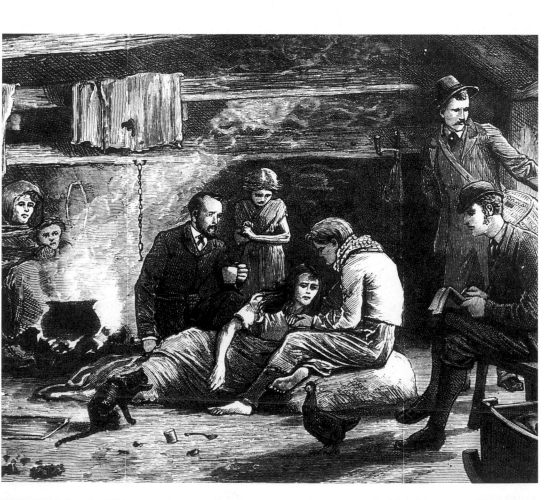

For the farm labourer who worked the land life was much harder. A cottage went with the job, but the condition of many of them was poor. The Dorset cottage in the picture is dated 1846 and certainly looks ramshackle. The roof needs repairing, as do some of the walls. The main problem for the labourers and their families was low wages. If you lived near a large town wages were higher, because farmers knew you might leave for a town job. But far away from the towns wages were very low. In Dorset in the 1850s, labourers were paid 40p a week. Not surprisingly their cottages had very little furniture or comforts.

One area of Victorian Britain that was still completely agricultural was Ireland. Here conditions for the labourers were even worse. In 1845 tragedy struck when the potato crop was destroyed by **blight**. The potato was the basic food of the Irish labourers and without it they starved. Look at the dreadful scene in this cottage. The family are thin, pale and starving. The woman in the centre is dying. No real help was sent and it is thought that 1·5 million Irish people died during the famine.

# HEALTH AND SANITATION

**Although the population of Britain rose dramatically during Victoria's reign, standards of health, especially in the cities, were not good. Hundreds of thousands of people living closely together led to unhealthy conditions. The threats to health came from bad housing, polluted air and poor *sanitation* – bad drainage and no real sewers. Also, when people became ill, health care was only available for the rich. A visit to the doctor was very expensive, so many ordinary people could not afford to go.**

▲ Cold, damp conditions in the home, combined with the filthy air of the industrial cities, led to tuberculosis – a highly *infectious* lung disease and the biggest killer of Victorian times. In Victoria's first year as Queen, 59,000 people died of the disease. A person who caught tuberculosis had a better chance of survival if he or she had access to clean air and a good diet. Not surprisingly, poorer people living in slum conditions of the type in the picture were most likely to catch it.

Sir JOSEPH BAZALGETTE CB
Engineer of the London Main Drainage System
and of this Embankment

▲ Another major killer in the nineteenth century was cholera. This terrible disease, which struck Victorian Britain many times, was caught if drinking water was *contaminated* by raw sewage. In towns and cities human waste was thrown into cess pits, dumps, streams and rivers, so clean water was very difficult to find. Joseph Bazalgette, whose memorial you can see, is one of the forgotten heroes of Victorian Britain because all his work lies underground!

◀ Bazalgette's sewage system, which opened in 1865, contained 131 km of underground sewers. The sewers took all London's human waste into huge tanks further down the Thames. When the tide went out, the sewage was released and taken out to sea. Huge steam engines, like the one in the picture, pumped pure water into the sewers and pipes that cleaned London.

# ENTERTAINMENT

**As you have learned, most people in Victorian Britain had to work very hard. They worked very long hours, six days a week. During the first half of Victoria's reign there was not much chance for free time. There were no holidays and the only day off was Sunday when everything was closed! Slowly things improved. Some workers were given Saturday afternoons off, and four Bank Holidays every year became law in the 1870s. With more time off and slowly increasing wages the opportunities for organized entertainment grew.**

▼ For most of the nineteenth century, the pub was a second home for many working people. In fact, many well-to-do Victorians were very concerned about drunkenness. They thought too much drink caused poverty and lawlessness. However, it seems that people drank because they were poor and living in such dreadful conditions. It was a way of forgetting their problems. Pubs were bright, lively places where company could always be found. Look at the 'Bull and Bush'. Can you read what attractions it had to offer? In 1875, on average, every man, woman and child in Britain drank over 160 litres of beer a year!

▲ The late Victorian period saw an increase in sports either to watch or take part in. The railway network allowed the creation of a Football League – teams and their supporters could travel long distances to play matches. Many modern day Football League teams date from the 1880s and 1890s. A sport that was very popular in the 1890s was cycling. Cheaper than buying a horse, bicycles were used to travel to work and to go out at weekends into the clean air of the countryside. There were 2,000 cycling clubs in Britain at this time with about 1 million members.

As we have seen, the railways created the ▶ seaside holiday or day-trip – a very important part of Victorian leisure. The rich could afford to spend up to a month at the seaside in the summer, and some well-off working people could stay for a week. The well-dressed holiday-makers in the picture are going for a pleasure trip, either into the countryside or to the coast.

Many well-to-do Victorians believed that *leisure* activities should be 'improving' or educational. This is why some rich people helped set up libraries, reading rooms, museums, concert halls and parks for people to use in their spare time. The Albert Hall in London, which is still used for concerts, was paid for out of the money made by the Great Exhibition of 1851.

Working people preferred the music hall, where for a few pennies they could watch a whole evening's entertainment. There were over 350 music halls around Britain and they were popular because of the warmth, light, company and humour. The songs and funny *sketches* were about people's everyday lives and were popular in a way that the 'soaps' on television are today. ▼

# EDUCATION

**The Victorian era saw a great interest in the education of children. In the early nineteenth century there was no law forcing children to go to school so many did not. Although the government provided money for church schools, they did not build schools themselves. By Victoria's death this had all changed. All children had to attend school by law until they were thirteen and the government had built many schools to provide places for all Britain's children.**

◀ The sons of the rich or well-to-do usually went to public schools. Most modern subjects were taught except science and practical subjects – these were not thought suitable for young 'gentlemen'. Look at the photo of Haileybury School. There are impressive buildings and huge playing fields. Public schools believed team games were an important way of teaching boys not to be selfish.

Schools for poor ▶ children were known as 'ragged schools', which you can see in the picture. The children are receiving their weekly free dinner. Their education was very basic – reading, writing and arithmetic, and Bible stories – which is why it was called 'elementary'. With big classes discipline was sometimes very harsh.

By the 1870s, the government was very ▲ worried about education in Britain. Other industrial countries were overtaking Britain and many people blamed the poor education system. Some, realizing that fewer children were working because of legislation, saw a need for more schools. In 1870, the government passed a law to build more elcmentary schools, called 'Board Schools'. You can see one in the picture. Is your school like this one? They were often very tall with big windows to let as much light in as possible. Ten years later attendance at schools was made compulsory. If parents failed to send their children to school they could be fined.

Keeping fit – called 'Drill' – was thought to be important, especially in city schools where health was often poor. Drill involved doing exercises when the teacher blew a whistle. ▼

# APPEARANCE

**Like many things in Victorian Britain, the clothes people wore depended on their position and wealth. The idea of fashion, particularly for women, was strong, mainly because the new railways allowed fashion ideas to spread more quickly. As a rule, the richer you were, the more ornamented your clothing.**

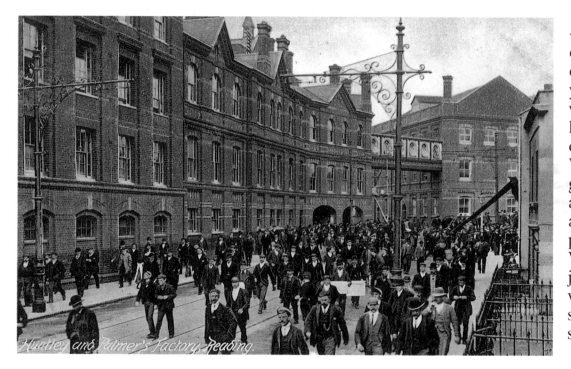

Huntley and Palmer's Factory, Reading.

◀ Look at the picture of a factory at the end of a day shift. It gives you a good idea of what working men looked like at the end of the Victorian era. What has every man got in common? They are all wearing either a flat cap or the very popular bowler hat. Waistcoats under jackets were common with a tie, but a white scarf usually hid a shirt without a collar.

Women's fashions changed a lot during the ▶ period. In the 1850s and 1860s well-to-do women wore a very strange fashion. Called the 'crinoline', it made women's dresses very wide and full. Look carefully at this woman having her crinoline mended. Can you see how it worked? The wooden frame was suspended from the waist and the dress hung over the top of it. The undergarments were called petticoats. Do you think this was a very practical fashion? What does it tell us about the everyday lives of these women?

26

◀ Look at the picture of the child crossing-sweeper. His job was to sweep a clear passage across the dirty street for rich people. He is poor and his clothes are torn. You may be surprised to see he is barefoot. This was quite usual for poor children as boots and shoes were expensive. The rich woman in her crinoline and silk bow does not seem to notice him. The group of men on the coach are wearing the typical clothes of prosperous Victorian men. Top hats (called 'stove pipes' – can you guess why?) and black frock coats with short waists and long tails were the mark of a gentleman.

It is interesting to ▶ compare the sweeper with this rich girl. She looks clean, well-dressed and cared for. Her dress is a child's version of the crinoline worn by women.

# SOCIAL PROBLEMS

**By the time Queen Victoria died in 1901, many British people were better paid, better clothed and fed, better educated and had more free time than at the start of her reign in 1837. However, it shocked middle-class Victorians to find out that between one-quarter and one-third of all British people lived close to or in poverty. Studies of London showed that for various reasons many people still lived without the basic necessities of life.**

Old age pushed ▶ people into poverty. If you were too old to work you did not get paid. The men in the picture are probably unemployed, cold and hungry and pay a penny to sit in a warm hall. The shelter has been provided by a charity.

The Victorians had struggled to overcome the problem of poverty, but with little success. In the early nineteenth century many rich people believed that people were poor because they were lazy. If they worked hard they would stop being poor. A law was passed saying that if a poor person wanted help they would have to enter a *workhouse*. These were usually unwelcoming and the conditions inside were deliberately harsh. Inmates had to wear a uniform, families were split up, food was basic and they had to work on boring jobs.

If you lost your ▶ job and could not pay your rent, you lost your home. The men getting ready for bed in the strange boxes are all homeless. Within seven years of Victoria's death, the government started to tackle this problem of poverty. In 1908 the first old age *pensions* were paid and soon after unemployment and sickness insurance were brought in. At last something was being done for the poor.

# GLOSSARY

**Blight**   A disease that makes plants wither and die.

**Compact**   Closely packed together.

**Contaminated**   Polluted.

**Engineering**   Designing and building large structures, including bridges, buildings and ships.

**Foundries**   Places where metals are produced.

**Historians**   People who study history.

**Industrial Revolution**   The huge change in Britain and other European countries during the eighteenth and nineteenth centuries from farming nations to industrial nations.

**Infectious**   A word to describe a disease that can be caught by other people.

**Leisure**   Time for enjoyment and relaxation.

**Parliament**   The ruling body of Britain.

**Pensions**   Payments made to people after they retire.

**Rent**   A regular payment to the owner of a building or land from the person who is using it.

**Sanitation**   Keeping buildings and the water supply clean so that they do not spread illnesses.

**Sketches**   Very short plays, usually funny.

**Tenant farmers**   People who rent land from a landowner and farm it.

**Textiles**   Cloths or fabrics.

**Ventilate**   To allow fresh air into a room or building.

**Viaduct**   A bridge that carries a road or railway.

**Workhouse**   A place where poor people did unpaid work in return for food and somewhere to stay.

# IMPORTANT DATES

**1837**   Victoria becomes Queen, aged eighteen.

**1840**   Victoria marries Prince Albert of Saxe-Coburg Gotha.

**1842**   Coal Mines Act forbids women and children under ten from working in mines.

**1851**   Great Exhibition in Hyde Park, London.

**1853**   Factory workers limited to ten hours work a day.

**1870**   Education Act. For the first time, schools are built by the government.

**1871**   Trade Unions are protected by law. First Bank Holiday Act gives four days holiday a year.

**1876**   Invention of telephone by Alexander Graham Bell.

**1878**   First cricket Test Match between England and Australia.

**1880**   Education made compulsory for all children between five and thirteen.

**1884**   All male householders given the vote.

**1889**   Charles Booth's survey *Life and Labour of the People in London* shows that nearly one third of Londoners live in poverty.

**1901**   Death of Queen Victoria, aged eighty two.

# BOOKS TO READ

**Daily Life in a Victorian House** by Laura Wilson (Hamlyn, 1995)

**Victorian Britain 1837-1901** by Andrew Langley (Hamlyn, 1994)

Wayland's **Victorian Life** series covers many aspects of the period, including work, clothes and school.

Heinemann's **Victorian Britain** books look at the whole period of Queen Victoria's reign, focusing on the Great Exhibition.

# INDEX